T0067233

The teachings of Brown Feather.

The Portal

in the park

JANIE ROSE

Author Credits: Reiki Master Teacher, strategic Interventionist, Nurse

Balboa Press books may be ordered through booksellers or by contacting:

Balboa Press
A Division of Hay House
1663 Liberty Drive
Bloomington, IN 47403
www.balboapress.com
1 (877) 407-4847

Print information available on the last page.

ISBN: 978-1-5043-8299-1 (sc)
ISBN: 978-1-5043-8301-1 (hc)
ISBN: 978-1-5043-8300-4 (e)

Library of Congress Control Number: 2017910035

Balboa Press rev. date: 06/26/2017

Contents

Dedication

I would like to take a moment to express appreciation to some special people in my life, for without them you would not be reading the words of this book.

To my dear friends Kathy Harter, and Tracy Nieskes Monteleone, and Margaret "Mags" Pagan. Thank you for seeing something in me I did not recognize as a gift. You told me I put you right in the stories I was sharing with everyone. Your words touched and inspired me beyond expression.

To Rita Coon, my dearest friend who put up with hours of reading, re-reading and helping me type pages to finish deadlines, and for your loving friendship and thoughtful encouragement on all levels. I am blessed. Thank you.

I give thanks to my spiritual teachers and guides, for assisting me with this human experience. For helping me to convey the message and blue prints for a joyous co-creative life for those who seek it. To live a beautiful, abundantly healthy, wealthy and fulfilling physical and spiritual life.

Last, but certainly not least, to my beloved Mother in Heaven. Through your trials and tribulations, you taught me to be fully present. To see, hear and feel all that surrounded me as I went about living day to day. To focus on each minute detail so that I was able to bring those precious details back to you. I was given words by the masters in such a way that you were able to ride the essence with me as though you were by my side. Your loss of the ability to walk and enjoy the outdoors, gave me the gift of writing. I love you so, and thank you for all that you gave me. Now you are unencumbered by your physical body that no longer served you. You are able to fly on angels wings to be by my side with the gifts that heaven blessed you with.

Chapter 1

The Farm

In the fall of 2005, my friend Sherri, a real estate agent, called us and told us of a great little farm that had not yet been officially listed on the market. My partner Meredith and our sons, Andrew, Christopher and Ryan, went to look at the farm. I stood at the top of the long, down-sloping driveway, my eyes scanning the lay of the land: trees and wildlife as far as the naked eye could see. Autumn had certainly put on its best dress to greet us. As Meredith and I looked out across the great Smokey Valley, aka Genesee River Valley, directly beyond the border of the farm, Meredith said, "I think I would love living here, Janie." She had walked about a hundred feet down the driveway, taking everything in, and now started back toward the boys and me.

I agreed with her. "Me too, Mer. It reminds me of when I was young, growing up on the farm in Brooks Grove."

I was actually a little shocked that my city-born-and-raised partner was loving the idea of farm life for our boys and us.

The fall foliage was at its peak, and that helped to cinch the deal for me. It was so vivid one almost needed polarized lenses to quell the brightness. The beauty and the crisp scent of the autumn leaves in the air were sheer delights to my senses. We fell in love with the farm and made an offer. It was accepted, but due to red tape, many months passed before we closed on it and our dream of owning it came to fruition.

One more signature, one more piece of paper, and so on, and so on. Yet something compelled me to keep pressing forward. Perhaps pure stubbornness. Who knows? Normally, it would have been beyond my level of patience, and I would have given up.

At long last, my pigheadedness paid off. I remember it like it was yesterday, that snowy March evening in 2006. My dad, Meredith, and I drove into Rochester, a good thirty-five miles, to sign the closing papers on the farm. Not just any farm, our farm. There were 117 acres of heaven on earth. I do not know why this farm was so different from any other; it just was. It called "home" to me as God would beckon his children home. There was a haunting feeling—like a pull in my gut, like a déjà vu—a familiarity and sense of belonging.

Spring erupted and dropped Mother Nature smack dab into our laps. Her plush, velvety gown of green covered the earth, with vibrantly colored drops poking their heads through in the shapes of crocuses, forget-me-nots, and every other wildflower you could dream of. Spring also brought with it my working papers. Having grown up on a dairy farm, I was no stranger to hard work and, thankfully, had a somewhat working knowledge of farm life. The farm, having not been worked in twenty years or better, had eight fields overtaken with weeds, saplings, and hundreds of English wild rosebushes. The rosebushes were over six feet tall; they went up past the top of the tractor's hood. All this bramble was certainly not going to let my hay crop grow.

We needed as much hay as we could muster because, you see, we had rescued five foals—two boys and three girls. We adopted them from a PMU foundation. PMU stands for pregnant mare urine. There are large farms that collect urine from pregnant female horses (mares) to manufacture synthetic hormones for humans. They are brutal. Many horses lose their lives. A significant number of the babies die when they are ripped away from their mothers and sent into the elements, barely able to survive with their mother's care, let alone without them. Many of the farms are in northern Canada and the Dakotas. These particular places are known for their harsh winters. Many animal cruelty prevention groups have tried to get these farms banned, but to my knowledge, little progress has been made in the closure of such facilities. One of the things promoting the continuation of pregnant mare urine (PMU) collection farms is the usage of synthetic hormone replacement therapy. As long as they are being prescribed, the pharmaceutical companies will keep producing.

The horses were on their way to be with us at their

forever home. We were so excited they would finally be here. We adopted them in the late fall of 2005. The horses stayed at the rescue farm in Canastota, New York, until we moved into Park Side Farm. It was hard having the horses at the rescue farm, as Canastota was over two hours away and made visiting our equine kids difficult. Having the horses there made Park Side feel like a real farm. Takoda (Ed), Finnian, Kacheena, Dulcinea, and Little Heart were their names.

I named our farm Park Side as it bordered Letchworth State Park on two sides. Letchworth State Park is my favorite place on earth. It's seventeen miles long, 14,350 acres, and has three amazing main waterfalls; there are fifty waterfalls throughout the park. The 550-foot-deep river gorge boasts the highest train trestle in the world.

Letchworth State Park had been home to the

Seneca Indians. The Seneca were the furthest west of the Iroquois confederation, the keepers of the western gate. William Pryor Letchworth, known to the Seneca as *Hai-WA-ye-is-tah* (man who does right thing), bought the middle falls area in 1859. This magnificent area became known as the Glen Iris estate and was Letchworth's home until his death in 1913. He donated the estate to New York four years before his passing but was granted life use of his beloved home.

Parkside had an amazing park-like setting and wildlife galore. The two ponds served as refuge for green heron, but they were more teal than green, if you ask me. They had bright orange feet and legs, a magenta underside, and a spear-like beak that allowed them to feast on fish.

A pair of Canadian geese returned each year to the upper pond. The large gray beauties sounded their familiar trumpets as if to say, "Hi, Janie, we are home," as they spread their wings and came gliding onto the water. Their webbed feet served as natural water skis; water shot out from all sides—swoosh! Without missing a beat, gracefully as swans, they began swimming about. *Honk, honk, honk*—they constantly scanned the perimeter of their aquatic home. Assuring no danger was lurking about and content that all was well, the incessant honking faded into a peaceful swim. Baby goslings—little balls of yellow and brown fur, orange feet and legs—were born with an innate sense to swim shortly after they hatched. Mama goose in the lead, the goslings were single file, close in tow. Bringing up the rear was papa goose Grisim. Being a goose caboose is an important job. The goose family stayed until the goslings could make the two-mile trek through the fields and woods to the river. Bless their little hearts, showing such perseverance at such a young age.

White-tailed deer came to the pond to drink and to nosh on the apples in the small orchard in the south yard. I especially enjoyed late spring when the does had their beautiful, little, spotted fawns in tow. Gosh, they were cute. Mama cautiously kept a watchful eye for predators, their white tails dancing and swishing about playfully. At other times, the tail acted as a warning signal, standing straight up, alerting the herd of impending danger.

With spring here and the arrival of the five horses, it was time to get to work reclaiming the hayfields. Thankfully, I grew up on a 250-acre dairy and cash crop farm in rural Western New York. It was my family's homestead and was then owned by my parents, Kenny and Betty Howe. I was the youngest of six children with sixteen years separating me from my oldest sister. I have three sisters, Barb, Vanessa, and Danise, and two brothers, Kenny Jr. (Ricky) and James.

I always loved helping Daddy. By the time I was nine years old, my legs barely long enough to reach the brakes and the clutch on the tractor, Dad had me help him with the fields. He always gave me the least dangerous tractor jobs, if you can call any farm machinery safe for a nine-year-old. Mother would have a fit every time she saw me get on the tractor, but Dad and I did not let that slow us down.

I learned everything I could from Daddy. I was always in his hip pocket. I adored him and was fascinated with, and always eager to learn, how to operate and fix machinery as needed.

My father was a handsome, charming man with dry wit and a gentle, loving way about him. His soothing words and big, strapping arms made me feel so safe and loved. There was not much of anything he could not make better.

My farm and mechanical abilities as well as my charismatic ways I owe to my father. Most of all, Daddy was a dreamer, my favorite trait I inherited from him. He was always coming up with some crazy idea on how to get rich quick. He had his own landscaping business once and a cycle shop where he introduced mopeds to the Nunda in 1979. His trust in people was larger than his wallet, unfortunately, and the businesses failed. My nursing talents I inherited from my mommy. And we kids got our musicality from both of our parents. Singing and playing guitar was one of my favorite things.

In 2003, I was seriously injured at my job as the head nurse on a dementia-Alzheimer's unit. A confused patient got tangled up in the cable wires behind a TV in his room. I heard one of my nurses call for help, and when I was assisting, the patient fell on me and snapped my neck, herniating and rupturing three discs. This injury ended my twenty-year career of nursing, so there was no going back to that. I was an awesome nurse, and it was, in my mind, who I was. Medicine just came naturally to me. My nursing and singing abilities defined me and were the sources of my confidence. The injury took away my nursing career, and a sudden onset of horrible panic attacks took away my singing ability. When I would get on stage, I suddenly started to hyperventilate, and soon the joy of singing was gone. The loss of my ability to share my talents began to create a self-loathing and bitterness within me. Not being able to nurse did, however, give me more time to putter around the farm, and that came in handy.

In mid-June, on a bright sunny morning, I set out on my maiden voyage to reclaim the land. Mounting my trusty steel steed, I began brush-hogging weeds towering over the hood of the tractor, which was at least seven feet high. I have to tell you it was a bit of a frightening adventure because I was driving into the unknown. I had zero knowledge of that land's condition. The gnarly weeds hid any large rocks or holes that might be present. My biggest fear was tipping the tractor over in a hole or on a boulder in the way. In the third field into my reclaiming, my fears were nearly realized when I came upon a four-foot-deep hole. Apparently someone had used a backhoe to dig up evergreen trees. My right rear tire sank into the hole, causing the tractor to start tipping over. Fortunately, with some good thinking and fancy driving, I recovered. Thank God my father taught me almost any situation one might encounter with farm equipment.

It took a good two weeks before I got all the fields

mowed. The work and time spent was well worth the effort. The sixty-plus acres of tillage land were now more like grassy meadows rather than a jungle of useless bramble.

My little family and I had a couple of good years on the farm together, but time always marches on, and indeed it did. Life kicked us repeatedly in the tuckass. Daddy, my best friend and mentor, became deathly ill. Having contracted a candida infection that went systemic, he eventually passed away from an infarcted bowel that rendered them nonfunctioning. Meredith had three surgeries in six months. She tore the meniscus in her knee, got gall bladder stones that required removal of her gall bladder, and then had cervical cancer requiring a total hysterectomy. And last but not least, my mother was diagnosed with stage-four colorectal cancer. All of this was in a year's time. Meredith and the kids, since they were biologically hers, moved out not long after my father's passing, leaving me alone on the farm with just the horses, barn cats, and dogs for company. Unable to cope with all that life threw at us, I became mean and self-loathing. I was an empty shell of who I once was. I hated myself so much that I spewed toxic waste on everything I loved—on Mer, the kids, everything that was important to me. I was just hateful. That hatefulness came at such a high cost.

Financially, things really started to crash. Without Meredith's full-time income from her job at the peanut butter factory to help supplement the household income, I found myself in active foreclosure. Tormented, I thought, *I cannot lose the farm.* I just could not! If I lost the farm, my equine kids would have nowhere to live. I could not bear to lose the horses. They had become my life. I showered every bit of love I had inside on them. Losing the dogs, the kitties, any of them would be unbearable. I had already lost so much.

Looking back, having the horses saved my life. I was at such a low point that I just didn't want to be here. However, having to get up and make sure all of the animals were fed and watered gave me enough purpose to survive.

Chapter 2

My Journey

Over the next couple of years, the horses and I did a whole lot of learning. They learned their purpose in being trained for trail riding. I too learned of my talents and gifts. Until that point, all I had known was nursing, singing in a band, and the farm.

In 2009, I was blessed with a new friend in my life. My sensei, meaning sacred teacher, Robin Wind. I met Robin through her business partner one afternoon in her shop in Rochester. I would say it was quite by chance, but I do not believe anything is coincidental.

I was so torn up at the turn of events—Dad's death, Mer leaving, and so on—that I thought there was bad energy in my house. So I hired Robin to come do a cleansing. She recognized I had psychic-medium gifts and invited me to come to a class to learn how to hone my gifts. I was nervous but more excited than anything and graciously accepted her invitation.

Sensei helped me to embrace the spiritual gifts I had long squelched, out of fear of them. I learned why it seemed I always attracted the sick, the lost, and the broken—not just people but animals too. I could pick a kitten out of a litter of seven, and that would be the one that ended up as the sickly one. I always found that a rather curious lot in life to bear, to say the least.

It seemed also I could be in the presence of a body and recognize its illness, be it physical or emotional. I just knew somehow they had a particular disease or condition. I thought it was a normal everyday occurrence, as my mother had this ability as well. Emotionally, if a person acted in a certain way, such as aloof, distant, a loner, or so on, I could tell why they acted the way they did. I could tell what the cause of their mental strife was (e.g., molestation or physical or emotional abuse).

I could think of a person, and soon that person would show up at the door, or the phone would ring and it would be them. I never realized these were gifts from God until I met Robin. Robin took me under her spiritual wing and helped me to understand these spiritual gifts rather than fear them. I am a medical intuitive, a psychic medium, and above all an empath and healer. I feel the joys and sorrows of others as well as my own. I can at times feel their physical pains before they tell me.

My mother's gift to me is to love with every ounce

of my being and with all that I am. It is risky business putting yourself out there like that, but the rewards of loving with that depth far surpass the risk of getting hurt. The idea of standing outside the fire is foreign to me and an idea that I cannot quite wrap my head around.

In the midst of the horses learning to be safe trail horses and my new journey, my friend Lori introduced me a spiritual teacher named Abraham - Hicks. Abraham brought the teachings of the law of attraction. The law of attraction is the law that governs the universe. In a nutshell, you attract what you dominantly think and feel. For example, if your dominant feeling is that of joy, you will attract more things into your experience that produce the feeling of joy. In the same token, if your dominant feeling is that of fear or worry, you will attract more things into your life that cause fear and worry. The law of attraction helped me to remember who I was. I was not the flesh, bones and blood I knew as Janie but my soul, the piece of God that illuminated my being. That was the authentic me. The remembrance of who I truly was gave me the ability to manifest the life I wanted. It brought joy, abundance, well-being, and peace into my life.

Part of the joy in my life was manifesting a wonderful trail-riding business and two new horses, Alo and Josie, along with a successful holistic center here at Parkside Farm. The rides went straight into Letchworth Park. In addition to those joys, my mother, Betty, came to live with me, which brought me even greater happiness.

Chapter 3

The Portal

It was getting on toward late October, and the trail-riding season was winding down for the year. I have always had a rough time transitioning from super busy to a roaring halt. I am not saying that there is not always plenty to do on the farm. There are things like cutting and splitting wood for the winter's warmth and winterizing the horse barn for the cold season. Then there is, of course, storing all the farm equipment and the necessary seasonal maintenance on them. There is definitely enough to keep you busy, but it is a different kind of busy.

Now the blessing of having Mom live at Park Side with me brought great joy. I enjoy her immensely; we laugh often and have such wonderful conversations about life in the olden times as well as modern events. Mom is very wise and insightful. She brings many different perspectives to many different things to ponder. Mom is wheelchair bound due to a faulty hip replacement, which causes her to require assistance with activities of daily living. This also kept me busy, just not the kind of busy I was used to.

One day in particular, I grew more and more restless. It was a balmy autumn day with clear blue skies and beautiful sunshine, so I figured I would saddle up one of the horses and ride down into the park. I knew there would not be too many more days like this before wet season came. I find riding horseback, especially in the park, meditative. It is a place where I can be fully present and mindful. Riding always recharges my battery and aligns me with my higher self. It is for food for my soul.

Little Heart seemed to be the most eager to go and the horse that would accompany me on my trek into the park. Little Heart is what you would call an Indian Paint horse. Sorrel and white with a perfect heart on her left side and another on her throat area, hence the name Little Heart. She is tall and lanky, amazingly bright, and probably the most intelligent of my seven equine kids. I saddled Heart up, and we started our journey. There was a slight chill in the air to this otherwise gorgeous morning. Autumn is my favorite season. The fall colors of brilliant red, yellow, and orange painted the hillside. The leaves were so fragrant, sweet, and fresh, so invigorating. If I could bottle it as a perfume, I surely would. There air was still, not much noise, with the exception of the rhythmic clippity-clop of Little Heart's hooves falling upon the well-packed trail beneath us. The occasional crow on the way tried to get his message across to one who was not fluent in blackbird messaging yet. Leaves rustled as a squirrel scurried to pack away a few more hickory nuts for his winter repast.

The trees were all heavily laden with fruits and nuts. In my experience, that has always portended a harsh, long winter. The park seemed to open her heart and welcome me to venture deeper into the depth of her bosom. We were entering areas that I had yet to explore. Trees, old, old trees that looked to be four or five hundred years old. Majestic matrons of the forest reaching endlessly toward the sky with a girth of six feet around. I was enveloped in their splendor, and my mind began to wander the way it often does. In quiet contemplation, I began to wonder what visitors these wooden souls might have encountered. Did a young Seneca warrior seek shelter beneath her motherly boughs? Perhaps Mary Jemison herself sought shade under this tree. Mary Jemison was the white woman of the Genesee. The Seneca Indian captive from the age of fourteen until her death at ninety-seven years old.

I felt warmth in my solar plexus as I pondered how much more simple life must have been in those olden days of yore. A time when there were no nuclear bombs, no airplanes flying into buildings killing thousands of innocent people. Food was clean, fresh, and unadulterated by chemicals and genetic modifications. Yes, there was the French and Indian War and the Revolutionary War, but still somehow it seemed to me it would have been more peaceful than today. Ah, the ride was just what the Reiki master ordered; I was already feeling my body and mind decompress.

I was pulled from the depth of my thoughts by Little Heart's apprehension about moving forward. She was on high alert, which caused me to be as well. She refused to go one more step forward. She began throwing her head and rearing up on to her hind feet. "What is the matter, girl? What is it? Whoa ... easy, baby." My attempts to calm her were an exercise of futility.

I looked about, thinking maybe she saw a rattlesnake. I had always heard the park had diamondback rattlesnakes, but thankfully, I had never encountered one personally. Finally, with much prodding, I got the horse moving forward once again.

I rounded the bend and came face-to-face with what Little Heart had already sensed. Standing there on its hind feet, waving its front paws, was a seven-foot black bear. The bear let out a loud growl, sending the already spooked equine over the edge. She reared up on her hind feet only to lose her footing on the loose stone, sending horse and rider careening backward into a large crevasse. The abyss seemed bottomless as we toppled and fell deeper and deeper. I remember thinking there was no way we would survive this kind of fall. Scenes from my life flashed before me as if frame-by-frame in slow motion, in addition to thoughts of Mom and how would she survive without me, as well as thoughts of the other horses and the farm. All of these things depended on my well-being. Who would take care of them if not I?

I hit my head on a large rock and lost consciousness. Much to my surprise, I did awaken, though I am not sure how long I was out. I quickly looked around for my beloved companion, Little Heart. Phew, there she was, not far from me. Oddly enough, she did not have a mark on her, thank God. She stood over me, sniffing and nudging me as if to say, "Okay, time to get up." Other than the bump on my head, we both seemed to be miraculously okay.

"Thank you, dear God, for seeing us to safety." I accepted the miracle. To say I was full of gratitude is an understatement.

I mounted back up on Little Heart. Intuitively, we headed in the direction I felt was toward home, but something was off. The air seemed more still, along with an almost deafening silence. I looked up to an empty sky, devoid of all air traffic. I had only beheld that eerie sight once before in my lifetime, September 11, 2001. It was an incredibly creepy feeling. What was going on? I wondered. I rode for what seemed an hour. Nighttime was falling quickly. There was no sign of a familiar trail or my woods in sight. How could this be? I had ridden these trails hundreds of times. *Maybe I hit my head harder than I thought.*

Chapter 4

Brown Feather

I started hearing random snaps of twigs and branches. I was worried that the bear might be following us. I quickly glanced around and did not see anything, and Little Heart seemed at ease, with no sign of peril. I chalked it up to being jittery from the bear incident. I relaxed back into my saddle, my heart still up in my throat. We continued onward.

With my eyes fixed on the trail ahead, much to my surprise a man stepped out of the bushes onto the trail in front of me. Squinting my eyes to get a better look at him, I could not believe what I was seeing: a full-costumed Seneca Indian brave. He was lean and tall, donned in buckskin pants and vest. His headdress had two red-tail hawk feathers and an emblem of a great blue heron on the headband. I remembered one of the Seneca clans to be heron. He was wearing authentic Seneca garb; I could say that much for him. *Must be a reenactment of sorts in the park*, I thought.

The brave said, “Brown Feather, where have you been, my brother? You have been gone many hours. We grew worried about you.” I recognize the name Brown Feather from my meet-and-greet spirit guides class with Sensei. He is one of my spirit guides—not just any spirit guide but my gatekeeper. The gatekeeper is the one who controls who and what is allowed into your aura. Still, why was this man calling me Brown Feather?

I decided to play along. After all, I was out in the middle of nowhere with this strange man who was dressed up for Halloween a little bit early. I was unsure of what his intentions were. Quite frankly, I was afraid. "I am sorry. We encountered some trouble," I answered.

"This I saw. My brother, you have blood on your head. What happened?" the brave questioned.

My brother? Why is he calling me his brother? I have been mistakenly called sir before when I've had a short haircut, but really, brother? Still, I decided to go along with him until I got things figured out or saw something familiar and could make a run for it.

"Come, Brown Feather. Let us get you home," said the brave.

I followed him down a path he seemed to know. I was clueless as to where we were and could not possibly find my way out of the park. We made our way through the forest, Little Heart, the brave, and I. I could not help but notice the number of elm trees we were encountering. Elm trees had all but died off over a hundred years ago from Dutch elm disease. What an amazing find. *Must be these trees were far enough into the park that they eluded the disease*, I thought. *How nice it would be to reintroduce them to our area.*

We stopped at a stream to let Little Heart quench her thirst. She had to be parched from the long ride. I knelt before the water to see if I could get a better look at the wound on my head in the reflection. I saw a head wound all right, but it was on someone else's head. The reflection looking back at me was not my own. It was not Jane looking back at me but the face of a very handsome thirty-something-year-old Seneca medicine man. I could tell I was a medicine man by the medicine stick and the pouch of herbs on my side. I had all of Jane's memories and mental awareness, but that was all that was physically still me as her.

The medicine man of the tribe was the communicator, healer, educator, prophet, and mystic. The tribe's sage advisor. I glanced at Little Heart; she looked the same. *Oh, my God, what is happening to me?* I splashed water on my face in a feeble attempt to wake up from this obvious nightmare.

"Little Heart had a great thirst," said the other brave.

"Indeed she did," I answered, realizing he just called my horse by her rightful name. I know I did not say her name aloud. This was really getting creepy. "How do you know my horse's name?" I asked with a nervous laugh.

The brave answered, "Why would I not know her

name? You have had her since her birth. We trained her together. Do you not remember this?"

I had no answer for him; if I did, it would be a lie. My heart raced in my chest with terror. I felt so frightened. *What is this all about? Am I dead? Am I dreaming? What?* I noticed the brave watching closely. He said, "Relax, my brother. The cut on your head is not that bad. There is no need for fear." He obviously assumed that was what my anxiety was about. Doing my best to compose myself, I stood there trying to not let on that I was clueless as to my current situation. I was completely disoriented.

We reconvened our journey and walked what I figured to be about two more hours. We ended our trek to the best of my estimation at Squawky Hill. Being 100 percent accurate was difficult, as it was now dark. With everything silhouetted in black against a midnight-blue backdrop, I could see the orange glow of a fire just ahead of us, and the faint smell of wood smoke was in the air.

Chapter 5

The Clan

We stepped out of the woods into a rather large clearing that revealed a longhouse constructed of elm bark and poles. We entered the structure and were greeted by many of the clan's people. They were all gathered around a center fire ring. Each member seemed to have his or her own tasks to perform. Some were tanning hides, while others were making headdresses, and others were storing away beans, corn, and squash for the winter fodder. The longhouse was divided into sections, giving each family member a place of ownership for themselves and their immediate family. Lengths of elm wood sectioned off each family cubicle. The thatched roofs of elm wood bark contained a center smoke stack to vent the smoke outside from the ever-burning fire. We received a warm welcome from the tribe. Many of the elders were telling stories around the fire. I remember hearing that wintertime was a great time of storytelling to make their day go by. Seneca are known for their great storytelling.

It was apparent by the warm greetings I received that I, as Brown Feather, held a position of great love and respect. I was asked by the many what had happened to my head and why I was gone so very long gathering my medicines. I had validation in that I was correct about being the tribe's medicine man. That actually made sense, as I have brought healing and medicine to each of my lifetimes, present day included. As I mentioned earlier, I am a healer.

I could only answer their query with what I knew to be true. "A great black bear startled Little Heart, and we fell backward into a big hole. I hit my head as we were falling. I lost consciousness, and I am uncertain as to how long I was out. I had been trying to find my way home when we happened upon my brother."

"Oh yes. Don-eh-ogawa was very concerned about his little brother and insisted on going out to look for you," said the elder female.

"It was unlike you to be so long, Brown Feather," said Don-eh ogawa. "I felt strongly you were in peril."

Just then, a beautiful young squaw called Star Dancing came up to me and wrapped her arms tightly around my neck. Looking up into my eyes tearfully, she said, "I was most frightened, my husband. I could not go on living if something were to become of you."

Husband? Oh, Lord. Things just got even more complicated. What was to happen now I had no clue. The situation was overwhelming, to say the very least, yet I could not help but feel a connection between Star Dancing and me—a kinship, a sense of familiarity and knowing when I looked into her eyes. My body covered with gooseflesh in her presence, telling me my soul recognized hers. I knew she was a part of my soul tribe even though my present-day mind could not remember her. My sensei, Robin, had taught me of these things.

A soul tribe is a group of souls that shares past incarnations together. In one lifetime, one might be your mother, and in another lifetime she might come back as your sister, but most often souls will stick together in one way or another in each lifetime. Robin Wind shared with me in a reading once that my present-day love and I were the epitome of infinity. Meredith and I had lived and loved many lifetimes together. I never doubted this to be true because Meredith and I had knowledge of one special past lifetime together. That posed a question: *if Star Dancing is that very soul that dances with mine from lifetime to lifetime …* A tender smile came slowly to my face as I contemplated the possibility. With all the things that built walls between us in present-day life, it would be nice to experience our love without conflicting egos looming over us.

"You must be tired, my love," said Star Dancing. She led the way to our section of the longhouse. There lying in a little fur bundle was a tiny baby. Star Dancing said, "Red Eagle looks more like you every day. One day he will be a great medicine man just like his father." I studied Star Dancing as she spoke; her chocolate orbs twinkled as the stars above. Her movements were graceful, as if dancing her way across the room. I saw clearly how she earned her name.

I gave her an acknowledging smile and said, "I am exhausted and need sleep." We lay down in a bed made of sticks and animal pelts. Star Dancing snuggled up to me with her head upon my chest and arm around my waist. Strangely enough, it was comfortable and reassuringly familiar. A warmth in my solar plexus and a peace in my heart swept over me. As tired as I was, I could not help but think about Mom, the horses, and the farm as I drifted off to sleep. I prayed, "Dear Creator of all that is, please keep my mama and babies safe. Please watch over them, dear God, and place divine protection around each one of them. I love them so. Amen."

Chapter 6

The Vision

Sleep came rather quickly to me. The dreams I was having seemed like they belonged to someone else. I was walking along old footpaths in what seemed like Letchworth. My feet were bare; in fact, much of me was bare.

I was Brown Feather. I was he. I was greeted on my journey by many different beings from nature, each taking turns escorting me along the way. I was remembering what each one meant as part of my totem.

The first animal to appear in my dream was

White Tail. I have always loved whitetail deer. The doe told me she had come to remind me to be gentle and to go gently toward my dreams and aspirations. She counseled, "Do not force things, Brown Feather, and let all flow with ease. Exercise kindness to all of earth's inhabitants, both two-legged and four, both great and small." The deer walked with me for some time.

I could hear the roar of the Genesee River in the distance as we made our way through the wooded areas.

The next escort was a wild turkey. Turkey explained to me that he had come to remind me to share the bounty of my harvest with my family and others. Turkey is closely related to the Earth Mother, and he was there to remind me to respect and care for the earth. "Give thanks to her for the crops and other things she provides to you to sustain life. Earth is a living, breathing, organic being and is to be treated as such. Honor her as you would your human mother, for she gives you much. Without her, you would cease to exist."

My final escort was a great blue heron, which incidentally is the symbol of Brown Feather's clan. The Seneca consider the heron medicine the most powerful medicine of all. Its presence assured me of my own medicine and its strength that has passed down through my many lifetimes. Heron shared with me that it is the king of the marshland. Its legs are long, and the longer its legs, the deeper it can fish. This relates to life itself. The heron often stands on one foot as it hunts in the water; this encourages balance and our earth connection. His gangly legs remind us that you do not have to be massive in size to maintain stability. Its sharp, pointed beak, analogous to a spear, is quick to pierce its prey. This suggests that you should readily spear life's opportunities as they present themselves.

At last, I arrived at my destination. I could see smoke up ahead. Upon closer observation, I saw a sweat lodge. This was where I would meditate and try to make sense of how I had landed in a time two hundred years before I was born—and most of all, why.

I entered the lodge and sat alone. I began taking slow, deep breaths—in through my nose and out through my mouth. I could feel my body relax and my mind clearing. I savored each delicious breath. My eyes closed. I quieted my mind. Any unwanted thoughts that came, I simply acknowledged them and released them. Deeper and deeper I relaxed into a state of knowing. Connecting with infinite intelligence, I sensed my spirit guides and invited them to join me. As gatekeeper, I asked that only those that had the intention for my highest and best be allowed into my energy. “Dear God, I ask for divine protection, head to toe, front to back, and side to side. Thank you.”

I asked my spirit guides, “Why am I here?” I was told I was to be a teacher. I am to plant the seeds of knowledge in the hearts and souls of Brown Feather’s lifetime. They reminded me of the present-day life of Jane and the talk of the end of times on Earth. Most importantly, I was sent back in time by the Creator to help save humankind from its greatest enemy, itself.

The Creator told me to teach all souls that would listen everything I had learned from my life in the twenty-first century. “Teach them of the law of attraction, spirit and ego, how to be a miracle worker, the matters of the Earth, and most importantly that the greatest gift to share is love.”

“Teach them with your heart, and you cannot fail,”

said my guides. "Go back to the tribe and tell them what you know. You are loved with an ineffable love, Jane, and you were chosen by the Creator himself to make these things better for the generations of souls to come after you. Aho." Aho is Native American for amen.

I awoke as the sun peeked over the horizon. The sky was alive with such brilliance. Purple, pink, orange, and red washed across the azure swath like a great healing blanket sent from the Creator to safely swaddle his beloved children. So beautiful. I took it as validation of the vision I had encountered in my sleep. It had to be a message from God, and I now knew my purpose as Brown Feather.

I first awakened the elders. I shared with them what Spirit revealed to me in my vision. The elders arranged for a council meeting, where it was determined I would deliver the knowledge I had acquired to the people of the tribe.

Chapter 7

The Teachings of Brown Feather

The Onodowa'Ga clans began to gather around a great fire. Wolf, turtle, bear, beaver, heron, hawk, snipe (a wading bird of wet or marshlands, beautifully camouflaged brown plumage), bear, and deer clans were there in great numbers.

"My people I have been given a message from the Great Spirit to teach you the laws of the universe so that many generations to follow us will know the truth. I am told that three hundred years from now, the people and the Earth mother will be in great danger. They will be on the brink of mass destruction. The world will go insane. The world will end as we know it, and humankind will lose its way. Darkness and illusion will blind them from the light within them. They will no longer know who they are.

"After centuries of abuse and neglect, the Earth Mother will grow angry, and she will retaliate. Much suffering will come to be because of her anguish. There will be devastating floods, forest fires, and the earth will quake. The weather will control the people. Men will shoot big fire sticks into the ground and bust through her crust and cause great damage and instability.

"Humankind will lose sight of the son-ship. They will see themselves as separate, separate from each other and from God. They will become strangers based on the color of skin, whom they choose to love, and by the God that they choose to worship; all will be judged by one another. They will think only of themselves. No longer will the tribe be as one. Worse yet, humans will become separate in their minds from the Great Spirit, the Creator of all things. They will lose sight of their own connection to their soul source energy, their belonging and oneness with all that is.

"We must do our part to prevent this from happening. Believe what I am to tell you. Listen with your heart and then pass this knowledge along to all you know and ever will know.

"The first thing you have to try to remember is that our soul or our spirit is energy and that Spirit came from the same source. Our soul is who we truly are. It is the God part of us, the part that is connected to infinite intelligence. Our soul is a piece of the Great Spirit that breaks away from the stream of knowledge and becomes physically manifested into being in the world. Our living as humans and sifting through all of the contrast that physical life offers adds to the expansion of the Creator as we know it.

"You will know if you are aligned with your soul source, as you will feel happy, confident, healthy, energetic, passionate, and inspired. When our lives are unfolding in the way we want them to, we can be assured of our alignment with Source.

"In the same token, when things are not going the way you would like, it just means most of your time is being spent worrying, living in fear, doubt, and a general feeling of lack. This law that governs the universe is known as the law of attraction. Simply put, like attracts like.

"The universe—or as we call it, God—is aware at all times what you are feeling and sends to you more things that match your most dominant feelings. If you spend most of your awake hours worrying or fearing starving from hunger, then you will not find enough to eat, and your crops will not flourish. If your most prevalent thought is you do not have enough pelts for the trading, then your trapping will not produce enough pelts. When you live in fear, you block the love from the Creator, his guidance, and all of the abundance that is yours. Abundant health, joy, and wealth are the rewards of living a life of connection with the Creator.

"The way to live the life you wish is to practice being grateful. You do this by training your mind and thinking the thoughts of positive expectations. Expect the best to come, and it will. Give prayers of gratitude for all the good things you do have. Sink deep into the thoughts of all that is right in the world and do this often. Do not give attention to unwanted things. Mentally list all that you feel appreciation for and say a prayer of thanks to the one who gifted you these things. Living in a state of appreciation, you truly are aligned with your source and thus keep bringing more good things into your life.

"Do not be afraid, however, when you notice a negative thought came into your mind of an unwanted thing. Just take a quick look at it and ask yourself, 'If this is an unwanted thing, then what is it I do want?' For example, if you noticed your bins do not have enough squash in them, it indicates that you want more squash. Turn your mind away from the lack of squash to the thought of the bins being full. Appreciate the abundance of them. Taste them in your mind. Revel in the good feelings of a prolific crop. Milk the good feelings as long as you can. By turning your mind from lack to abundance, abundance is what you will get. Trust, believe, and expect it without doubt, and you will see it come into your life.

"Energy is a vibration, and everything has its own vibrational frequency. God is the highest and fastest vibrational frequency there is. Our feelings or emotions have their own vibration frequency as well." Picking up my guitar, I went on, "Just like the strings on my guitar vibrate. The low notes vibrate very slowly, and the high notes much faster. Think of God way up high in the sky. The high notes are much closer to God because God's vibration is fast and high. The low notes are closer to earth and are more human-like.

"Positive feelings like joy, passion, hope, and elation are high notes closer to the frequency of God, and negative emotions like fear, anxiety, depression, frustration, and pessimism are slow moving and not near the frequency of God. When your frequency is low, you are attracting the unwanted things you are feeling. We as humans often spend time concentrating on fearful, worrisome things. Have you not ever noticed the things you worried about the most are often the very things that happened?

"You may say, 'Brown Feather, if I do not worry, my family and I could starve or freeze to death. If I care, I worry. I only care about the things my family needs to survive.'

"I say to you, what did you accomplish with all that worry? Did you have a better crop? Did you bag more game? No, I say your worry did not do either. All the worrying did nothing for you but nearly cost you the lives of you and your family. Your crop was meager at best and your quarry barely enough to sustain you.

"If you trust with all your heart that the Creator will provide you with all you wish for, it has to come; it is law. Once you ask for the wanted thing, cast all doubt aside and know it will be so. Live as though it has already come to pass. This is positive expectation. You never will lack for anything when you live as if you have everything. If you start to doubt that what you have asked for is coming, stop the thought right away and shift your thoughts to something that is pleasing to you. Thoughts of whatever feels better. If you truly do this, then I promise you, you will live a joyous, abundant life.

"Do not fight against unwanted things. If something you see displeases you, stop and ask yourself what that displeasing thing causes you to want. Maybe you look upon a field of corn that is drying up and dying. Looking at the unwanted drought makes you long for rain, does it not? Then turn your mind to the idea of rain. Dream of how wonderful it feels against your hot skin, cooling. See in your mind how luscious and green the rain makes all the crops and the grass. See all things flourish from the gentle fall of water from the sky. Appreciate how it quenches the thirst of all living things. Nurture how you feel and milk that amazing feeling for as long as you can. It will help bring the rain by sending a vibrational smoke signal to the Creator.

"The more time you spend finding things to appreciate, the more things you appreciate will come to you. Fearful things will bring in turn more things to feel fearful about. Your feelings will always be matched by more of the same. Love gets love, hate gets hate, lack gets lack, and abundance gets abundance.

"I hope, my people, that you take to heart what I am saying to you. I have great love for you, and my want is for you to live happy, healthy, joyous, abundant lives of ease. Aho."

Chapter 8

The Transformation

Winter came with a fury. The unforgiving winds of winter raged through the great canyon of the east. Mother Nature was taking no prisoners. The tribe hunkered down as best we could. The snow dumped feet upon us, making hunting and fishing difficult. I sensed all were silently thinking the same fearful thought: would we have enough provisions to see us through until springtime?

We sat moping in unison until something triggered my thoughts to what I was sent to teach my people. *Change my way of thinking from the lack and see to what it is I want.* I begin to pray aloud:

"Dear God, thank you for the food we have. Thank you for having enough. I appreciate how the food tastes and how it nourishes my body so that I may be a strong servant of the light. I love the warmth that the fire brings. Thank you, God and the trees, for your sacrifice so that my family and I are comfortable. I trust that all is well. Aho."

In the winter months, the tribe began going through

an amazing transformation. The crops were plentiful, and the hunted game was more than enough to feed each and every person well into the spring. The abundance overflowed. The tribe was happy and lived in a state of appreciation, thankful for one another and for all that the Creator had bestowed upon them. They no longer complained about a lack of anything. They kept their minds off of unwanted things, just as Brown Feather had taught them. The energy was alive and became more positively focused, more joyous with each passing day, as did my love for my people and especially Star Dancing and our son, Red Eagle.

Chapter 9

Star Dancing

In many ways, the twenty-first-century me, Jane, is a newborn in regards to metaphysics. In the present time, I have an amazing teacher. Thank God for my sensei, soul tribe family member, mentor, and dear friend Robin. She is a gifted pastor, medium, shaman, and Reiki master teacher. She has taught me so much and helped me tap into my spiritual gifts.

One of the things that stuck out in my mind the most was that when Robin spoke of my ex-partner, Meredith, the one I bought Park Side with, Robin saw the symbol for infinity, the sideways figure eight.

Robin told me that Meredith and I spent many, many lifetimes together. Our love for each other was a love that transcends time and space.

With Star Dancing, I felt the same soulful pull making me gravitate toward her. From the first instance of our initial encounter, I remember even then how familiar it felt being in her energy and how deeply and quickly we were connected to each other. A soul does not recognize another by its physical appearance but by the energy felt between them. I have always felt the eyes are the window to the soul. If I truly want to know a person, it is in the eyes I will find their authentic, unadulterated self.

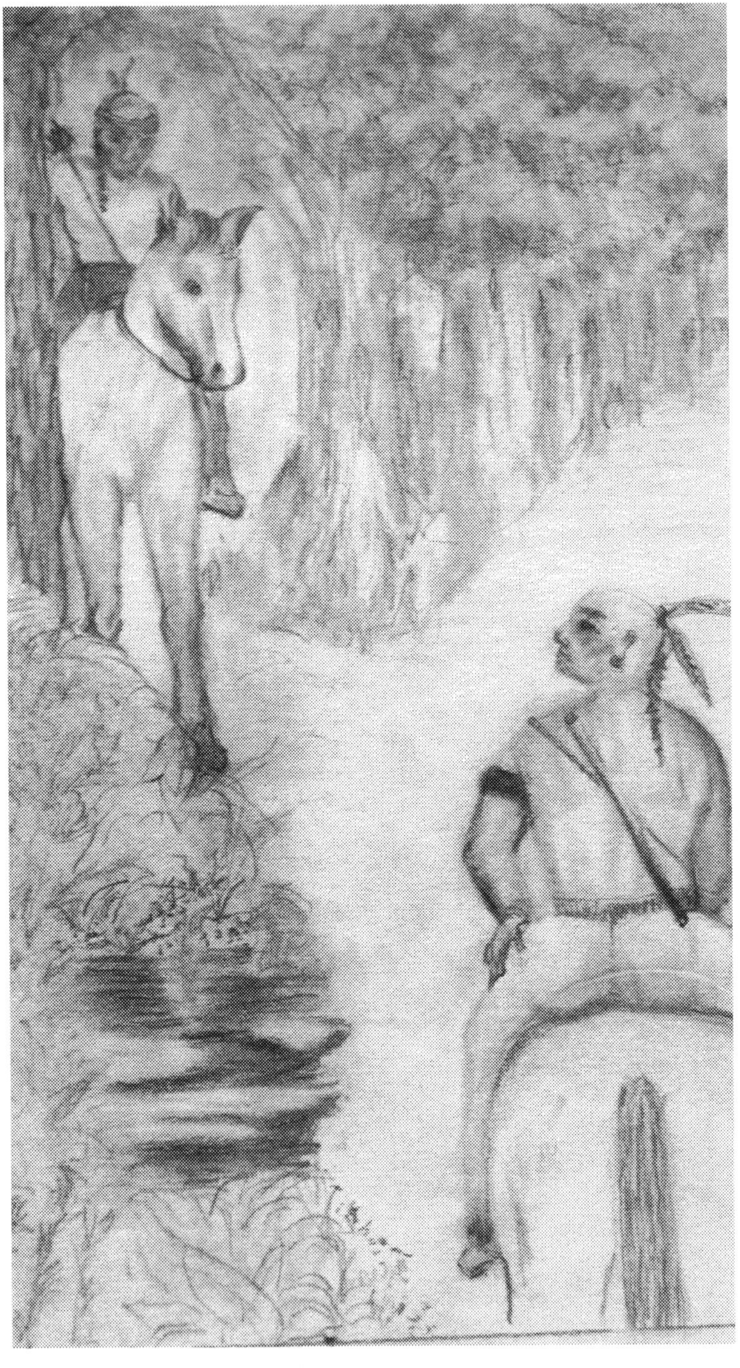

I was overwhelmed by everything that had happened at our first meeting. I was unable to comprehend what truly was going on. I only knew that Star Dancing felt comfortable to me in a very uncomfortable situation.

I begin to see and feel similarities between present-day Meredith and Star Dancing. At times when our eyes met and our gazes met, I could hardly breathe from the intensity of the chemistry between us. Because of the great love she had for Brown Feather, I was extra careful not to hurt her. I could not reject her, for she would not understand. I was still having trouble understanding that my soul was around Brown Feather's soul. How could I be in his body and still be Jane? All thoughts are vibrations, and every thought is eternal. I could somehow be physically connecting to his thoughts and the essence of who Brown Feather is and the life he led. The hole must have been some sort of time portal. That was the only thing it could be—the only thing that made even remote sense.

Walking hand in hand with Star Dancing along the bank of the Genesee River, we talked of many things, every now and again stopping to take in the view of the gorgeous Genesee Valley.

"It is cold, Brown Feather. Please hold me," said Star Dancing. She stepped into my arms and slid her hands inside my shirt to warm them, her fingers like feathers upon my skin, causing a ripple of electrical charge through my body, awakening the wanting in this body. Our eyes met as we leaned into each other, our lips finding one another's, a prelude to the most beautiful, loving, passionate kiss I have ever known. She murmured, "I love you," against my lips.

I softly whispered, "I love you too, Star Dancing." This kiss solidified my thoughts that Star Dancing was without a doubt Mer. I could now add the knowledge of another lifetime. Oh how I wanted to share with Star Dancing the facts about our future incarnation together. I wanted to warn her of impending harm that she would one day encounter, but I was not getting validation from Spirit to do so. Sensei always taught me, "Just because you can doesn't mean you should." I always say a prayer for the highest and best for all concerned before I give a spirit message. If do not get validation from Spirit to give the message, then I do not say anything.

We all have life lessons and karmic resolutions to achieve. I have learned you must let people have their own process and journeys to accomplish their soul's needs. Star Dancing had hers, and I needed to let her experience them even if it hurt, which in turn hurt me. It was difficult to look upon and say nothing. That has always been one of the hardest things for me, not being able to share what I intuitively know with people I love.

The spring and summer months to follow were the most amazing days of my lifetimes. So much love, joy, and laughter. The joyous times were beyond compare. Anytime I was with Star Dancing, all was right with the universe. To love and feel so incredibly loved in return was something I had longed for back in the future life on the farm. Life was so much simpler here, with nothing to fight about. No lack—only abundance of all things. The thoughts of my present-day life began to dim as I sank deeper into the contentment of the life of Brown Feather. Along with my personal joy came the joy of my people as they learned to live in appreciation and adopted the teachings I shared with them at the great ring of fire.

Chapter 10

The Healer

As Star Dancing and I made our way back to the longhouse, we were greeted by one of the braves saying I was needed right away, that my father, the chief, had been stricken with a great sickness.

As we entered the chief's cubicle in the longhouse, I found him to be mostly unresponsive. His lungs were full of congestion with wheezing and rattily respirations. I estimated his temperature to be 103 degrees Fahrenheit if not more. I knew in an instant that he had contracted pneumonia. In those days, pneumonia was more often than not a death sentence. I told the brave that the chief was very ill and we needed to act quickly.

I sent him to fetch icy-cold Genesee River water while I ran to my section of the longhouse to grab my medicine bag. It was a crude pouch made from tanned deer hide. The pouch contained all of the herbs, berries, and tree barks I had collected. I returned to the chief's bedside. Kneeling, I began to pray to summon my Reiki medicine. "Dear Creator of all that is, ascending masters, elders, and those who walk in the white light of God, I ask for your help and guidance in this healing of the great chief. Make me a pure, loving vessel in which for you to flow. Aho."

Placing my hands on his head, I felt my hands turn icy cold, for that is what his body needed to reduce the fever. I felt the presence of my healing guides as my body shivered with goose bumps. The hair on my arms and back of my neck stood on end. My hands were pulsing as if I had a heart beat in the center of my palms. In the center of my chest, I could feel a pulling sensation in my heart chakra. All of these were familiar sensations that I was receiving God's energy and the recipient of the healing was receiving it as well.

I muddled thyme, oregano, onion, and garlic into a paste and rubbed it on the bottom of his feet and on his chest. The sole of the foot is one of the thinnest areas of skin on the body and allows for rapid absorption of Ayurvedic medicine.

The brave returned with the cold river water. I soaked strips of cloth in it and placed them in his underarms, groin creases, forehead, and the back of his neck in an attempt to break his dangerously high fever.

I sat vigil at his bedside all through the night.

The morning sun brought a little improvement, but the fever still raged on. I knew in my heart of hearts if I could not get the fever under control, he was not going to make it. Getting water into him was not an easy task, and he was profusely dehydrated. The tiny spoonfuls I was getting into him were inadequate. I took white birch bark from my medicine bag, remembering it had salicylates in it. Acetylsalicylic acid is aspirin. Aspirin is used for pain and fever, I knew from my days of nursing. I had nothing to lose and everything to gain by trying.

I steeped some birch bark into a tea and ladled it into the chief in great hopes it would break his fever. I also muddled some mint leaves and rubbed the oil from them on his head and the bottom of his feet. I then ground mustard seed fine, made a plaster with animal fat, and rubbed it all over the chief's chest. I made warm a deer hide near the fire and placed it on the chief's chest to open the pores and allow the mustard plaster to penetrate deeper. The mustard plaster would loosen up the mucus in his lungs and help him to expectorate the phlegm, enabling improved air exchange.

By nightfall, the chief's fever had at last broken, and he started coming around. He was able to sip on broth and get some water into his belly. I religiously placed Reiki energy on the chief twice a day along with the herbs and plasters for two more weeks. He grew stronger with each new sun. At the end of the two weeks, my father was strong enough to resume normal living. I prayed, "Dear Creator of all that is, thank you for healing our great chief and thank you for the many gifts you gave to make this healing successful. Aho."

Chapter 11

The Harvest

Autumn was upon us, and with it came the harvest. What an amazing sight. Everything was aplenty. Three ears of corn on every stalk, bushels upon bushels of squash, beans, and corn. Why, there was enough to feed the clan two winters over. Physical manifestation of the abundance all about them was the only proof the clansman needed to believe that what I had taught them was truth.

The joy was so strong it was palpable. All of the tribe members were so elated and filled with passion for life. I felt I had indeed fulfilled my purpose, or at least part of it. It would be difficult to know if things changed in the present day where I was from. I was curious to know if I would ever get back to the twenty-first century to experience the fruit of the harvest of the seed of change I had sown in this lifetime as a Seneca Indian. I indeed hoped so.

I felt it appropriate to instill the importance of appreciation. “My brothers and sisters, please gather around. Let us give thanks and appreciation for the bounty that God bestowed upon us.

“Dear Great Spirit, Creator of all that is, we thank you for all that you have blessed us with the bountiful harvest and in living every day. May this food bless and nourish our bodies so that we are strong, capable servants of the light. Aho.”

Chapter 12

The Stranger

A man that wore a bright red coat and spoke with a foreign tongue visited our clan. He came asking for our support for the French Army and the New World colonists. He made promises of many riches if we would lend support. The Onodowa'Ga were a peaceful, loving tribe. I counseled our chief and reminded him that we would not help our tribe by fighting against anything; all that would do was bring more unrest and violence.

He heeded my advice with remembrance of how

my teachings rang true in the bounty of the harvest and how abundant we all were as a result.

Chief Corn Planter alerted the British soldier that we would not be joining their forces. At this, the man in the redcoat took his leave.

Chief Corn Planter did his best to stay true to his pledge of neutrality; however, a number of our clan were murdered as they were innocently looking upon the raging battle about us. This provoked the Onodowa'Ga to join, fighting with their fellow brothers of the Iroquois confederation against the French. I did my best to stay clear of the battlefront, doing my part by treating the sick and wounded with my ancestors' medicines. Since Star Dancing was great with child, I stayed as close to her as possible. The battle raged closer and closer. The French troops were moving in.

I took Star Dancing and Red Eagle deep into

the river gorge amongst the trees and made them a lean-to with enough provisions to last for a few months. I did this with the hope of removing them from harm's way. The attempt to ensure their safety was futile. We had been followed. A group of French soldiers started toward me. I was far enough away from the lean-to that perhaps they did not see it. I began running as fast and as far as my legs would carry me. I heard muskets being fired. I could hear the lead balls whistling past my ears. *I just have to save them,* was all I could think. *Oh my loves. "Dear Creator, I beg for divine protection for my wife, son, and unborn child. Please, dear God, let them live and let them know I love them so deeply and completely. Aho."*

Another shot ring out, and accompanying it was an incredible deep pain within my back, falling me to the ground. It was as though I was falling in slow motion. Flashes of my life there with my people, my son and my love flooded my mind and vision. "Oh God!" I screamed. *No! I have not gotten to see my unborn child. I'm leaving my children without a father to love and protect them.* "Star Dancing, I love you!" I shouted as everything faded to black.

The last thing I heard was Star Dancing screaming, "Brown Feather, no! I will always love you …"

"Jane! Jane! Jane!"

I opened my eyes to find my nephew Casey kneeling at my side.

"Grandma called me and said you had gone out for a ride hours ago and had not come back. She was worried," Casey said. Casey is my forty-three-year-old nephew who is only nine years younger than I. He is more like a little brother than a nephew, as he practically grew up with me at my parents' home.

Casey explained, "Then when Little Heart came

back without you, we knew something had to be wrong. It looks like you hit your head pretty good there." Casey helped me to my feet. "Little Heart has a few scrapes, but she'll be okay."

"What happened? Where am I?" I said.

"You're down in the park. Let's get you to a doctor. You must have been out quite awhile. It's pretty near dark." Casey helped me to mount my boy Finny, and then he mounted Ed, and we headed back to the farm.

Casey took me to the local hospital emergency room, and they performed all kinds of tests, including a cat scan, on my head and found no injury to my brain. Not even a slight concussion was detected.

Having ruled out any physical explanation for my experience, I immediately consulted Robin.

After telling Robin the entirety of my story, she validated it was indeed the revisiting of a past incarnation of mine. I was Brown Feather in that lifetime, and that is the reason I have such powerful medicine this lifetime. It was why Letchworth Park has always felt so familiar and safe to me. It was my home.

I shared some of this with Meredith. Some of it resonated with her as well. As for a reconciliation, we have cultivated a beautiful friendship and learned from our past mistakes. Time will only tell what the future holds for us. As for now, I am enjoying my friend.